Once Upon A Dream

Creative Reflections

Edited By Lynsey Evans

First published in Great Britain in 2024 by:

Young Writers
Remus House
Coltsfoot Drive
Peterborough
PE2 9BF
Telephone: 01733 890066
Website: www.youngwriters.co.uk

All Rights Reserved
Book Design by Ashley Janson
© Copyright Contributors 2024
Softback ISBN 978-1-83565-832-1
Printed and bound in the UK by BookPrintingUK
Website: www.bookprintinguk.com
YB0607P

FOREWORD

Welcome Reader, to a world of dreams.

For Young Writers' latest competition, we asked our writers to dig deep into their imagination and create a poem that paints a picture of what they dream of, whether it's a make-believe world full of wonder or their aspirations for the future.

The result is this collection of fantastic poetic verse that covers a whole host of different topics. Let your mind fly away with the fairies to explore the sweet joy of candy lands, join in with a game of fantasy football, or you may even catch a glimpse of a unicorn or another mythical creature. Beware though, because even dreamland has dark corners, so you may turn a page and walk into a nightmare!

Whereas the majority of our writers chose to stick to a free verse style, others gave themselves the challenge of other techniques such as acrostics and rhyming couplets. We also gave the writers the option to compose their ideas in a story, so watch out for those narrative pieces too!

Each piece in this collection shows the writers' dedication and imagination – we truly believe that seeing their work in print gives them a well-deserved boost of pride, and inspires them to keep writing, so we hope to see more of their work in the future!

CONTENTS

Bysing Wood Primary School, Faversham

Lexi Waller (9)	1
Tia Haynes (10)	2
Lilly-Rose Llewellyn (9)	4
Alfie Pioli (10)	5
Harlen Folse (10)	6
Lily-Grace Wiley (9)	7
Ikmat Mayungbe (10)	8
Shakil Boakye Ansah (10)	9
Shanvi Shandilya (9)	10
Toby Brown (10)	11
Dylan Jul-Ellison (10)	12
Max Speed (9)	13
Oscar Pilbeam (9)	14
Abiola Ogunneye (10)	15
Roman Reeves (10)	16
Ruby-Lou Adams (10)	17

Hadley Learning Community - Primary Phase, Hadley

Blanka Cichon (7)	18
Aleeza Arhbab (8)	19
Bethany Cocker (8)	20
James Grant (8)	21
Sienna Bowen (7)	22
Katriel Emiantor Itetia (8)	23
Julia Talmacel (7)	24
Dawood Usman (8)	25
Kikeé-Anne Mea (8)	26
Naysa Bhatt (8)	27
Kirandeep Swali (8)	28
Eliza Qasim (7)	29
Sydah Fathima (7)	30

Bilal T Mumuni Musah (8)	31
Carly Galbraith (8)	32
Lacey Edge (8)	33
Ivy-Rose Bryant (8)	34
George McDougall (8)	35
Lily-Mae Smart (7)	36
Owais Arif (7)	37

Hungerford Primary School, Hungerford

Beatrice Hewitt (8)	38
Akshar Patel (8)	40
Mia McGowan-Bailey (8)	41
Elodie Head (8)	42
Ava Cadle (8)	43
Elsie Taylor (8)	44
Jackson Bah (8)	45
Ronnie King (8)	46
Aaron Adam (8)	48
Lillie Smith (8)	49
Harvey Thomas (8)	50
Maria Vacareanu (7)	51
Frank Smart (8)	52
Imogen Giles (7)	53
Caitlin Roff (8)	54
Indianna Sandell (8)	55
Olivia Browning (7)	56
Lewis Berry (8)	57
Isabella Atkins (7)	58
Cody Lee (8)	59
Riley Blanchard (8)	60
Tommy Taylor (8)	61
Jamie Greenslade (8)	62
Frankie Sprules (8)	63
Gwynnie Binns (8)	64

Harrison Martin (7)	65
Ella Baker-Hill (8)	66
Luca Westbrook (8)	67
Sophie Armstrong (7)	68
Zoë Potolo-Rees (8)	69
Jackson Southwell (8)	70
Norbet Kroker (8)	71
Bailey Charman (7)	72
Amber Duca (8)	73
Henry Ellis (7)	74
Ted Thatcher (7)	75
Hermione Allard (8)	76
Louanna Annetts (8)	77
Will Cassidy (8)	78
Millie Taylor (8)	79
Aria Armstrong (8)	80
William Fisher (8)	81
Ava Kirby (7)	82
Oscar Hall (8)	83
Oliver Day (8)	84
Nicole Buck (8)	85
Jaxon Pavier (8)	86
Arya Little (7)	87
Jax Haines (8)	88

Killisick Junior School, Arnold

China-Rose Henry (10)	89
Georgia Poyzer-Green (10)	90
Oheneba Opoku (10)	91
Grace Fearnley (10)	92
Beatrice Ho (9)	94
Joanna Onyeso (10)	96
Atia Morrell (9)	97
Kennedy Mason (10)	98
Lu Chen (10)	99
Cherish Chan (10)	100
Kian Scott (10)	101
Jemima Onyeso (10)	102
Lois Camfield (9)	103
Cain Morrison (10)	104
Khloe Mitchell (9)	105
Oliver Wilkinson (10)	106
Jeremiah Onyeso (10)	107

Blessed Chipandambira (10)	108

Lakenham Primary School, Norwich

Arlind Kullaj (9)	109
Freddie Seal-Coon (9)	110
Dali Cooper (9)	112
Noah McCloy (8)	113
Charlie King (9)	114
Sophia Chapman (9)	115
Lola-Mae Smith (9)	116
Mollie Molloy (8)	117
Cameron Bamber (9)	118
Nanthitha Lenin (9)	119
Eleanor Quinlan (9)	120

Stechford Primary School, Birmingham

Zakaria Shah (9)	121
Mohammad Zain (9)	122
Falak Kamran (9)	123
Muhammad Musa Umer Binyameen (9)	124
Aizah Fatima (8)	126
Anayah Alam (9)	127
Daniel Vaughan (8)	128
Aariz Bin Haroon (9)	129
Ruqayyah Hussain (9)	130
Rumaisa Ansar (9)	131
Aleeza Arzu (9)	132
Yasmina Hashemi (8)	133
Zorian Khan (9)	134
Haleema Ahmad (9)	135
Muhammad Ukasha Ali (9)	136
Ali Awan (9)	137
Adam Hussain (9)	138
Divine Djala (9)	139
Isa Hussain (9)	140
Saima Rehman (9)	141

Sutton Manor Community Primary School, Sutton Manor

Minnie Hamilton (9)	142
Esmé Wright (9)	143
Billy Sutton (8)	144
Phoebe Langley (8)	145
George Mellor (8)	146
Esmee Dyer (9)	147
Hayley (9)	148
Oliver Craig (9)	149
Lexi Atherton (9)	150
Athisha Kopinath (9)	151
Sofie Veseia (9)	152
Marley Kelsall (9)	153
Elliot Kovac (9)	154
Mia Mohamed (9)	155
Rowan Fletcher (9)	156
Ethan Marsh (9)	157

West Denton Primary School, West Denton

Joseph Hanson (11)	158
Casey Reynolds (11)	159
Jaklyn Elizabeth Jinto (11)	160
Denver Bell (11)	161
Harley Mitchell (11)	162
Lola Jones (10)	163
Evie Richmond-Atkin (10)	164
Leila Birkett (11)	165
Charlie Johnston (11)	166
Sophie Thompson (11)	167
Sophia Calvert (10)	168
Alfie Grey (10)	169
Omasirichim Oparah (11)	170
Layton Ellis (11)	171
Rosie Rooney (11)	172
Jake Stoddart (11)	173
Katie McGuinness (11)	174
Yafee Ahmed (11)	175
Freddie Coulson (10)	176
Leo Dunn (9)	177
Freya Ions (11)	178

Frazer Branscombe (11)	179
Mason Barwick (11)	180
Ahmed Ayalu (10)	181
Darci Jones (11)	182
David Sager (10)	183

Whitestone Primary School, Swansea

Gabi Sidoli (10)	184
Judah Scott (11)	185
Dakota Mitchell (10)	186
Gwen Stephens (9)	187
Rajan Parmar (10)	188
Prabash Dissanayake (10)	189
Lilly Bromham (11)	190
Nell Taylor (11)	191
Lamar Haj Basheer (11)	192
Ella Evans (10)	193

THE CREATIVE WRITING

Clowns And Balloons

C lowns hunting in my home looking to play,
L oving my dog as the dog growls,
O nly flashing in the hallway, never been done,
W hen I came out of my room, the red clown came up,
N ervously, a clown chased me, so I took off,
S ometimes, I saw balloons, so I normally popped them,

A ndy, my next-door neighbour, waved when he was walking a balloon,
N ever happened before but he walked like a zombie
D og then ran next to me - "Go, go get them!" clowns laughed,

B *ish, boom*, slapping my feet as I ran hastily,
A s I cried, I ran to my friend's home,
L ooking at the gloomy sky,
"L eaving already?" a clown sighed,
O nce, then twice, I shook my head,
O nly to pop the balloon,
N ow, I ran! I obviously got lost, but I saw something,
S hould I put my dog in the abandoned home?

Lexi Waller (9)
Bysing Wood Primary School, Faversham

Dream Home

Drowning in the silence,
Struggling to sleep,
I tossed and turned,
Sparkling lights of rainbow colour,
Danced across the room,
Am I dreaming?
No, stretching out my hand,
I touched the light...
The light expanded across the room,
Glitter leapt into the air,
Jumping to my feet and waking up my friends,
As my hand grabbed for the door,
Too slow, too quick,
It pulled me and my friends in,
Whirling around I grabbed Dokie's hand,
She grabbed for Cheyanna's
Cheyanna grabbed for Eliza,
Down, down, down we fell,
Peculiar, I know, I thought of a dragon,
Suddenly... a dragon appeared,
Wow! I can control my dreams,
He was gaining on us all,
Bang went the hammer,

Imagine, imagine...
Imagine the way home,
This is enough we need to go...
Home!
The ground began to shake,
Things disappearing,
Finally, we were safe,
We were... home!

Tia Haynes (10)
Bysing Wood Primary School, Faversham

Nightmare

In one dream there were clowns and zombies,
Until I fell to the depths and stopped,
Wandering around by Lexi's side
Feeling trapped inside
Then I realised the clowns had caught me,
There were spiders on my face,
That's the last time I saw Lexi,
Pulling the spiders off my face,
I searched for Lexi not knowing what was behind me,
Waking up to screaming which distracts the clowns,
I woke up with Lexi by my side, asleep,
Running away I forgot about Lexi,
I knocked the clowns and got Lexi,
Looking behind me where the clowns were chasing us
Being dragged by Lexi walking out of the abandoned building,
Going home to see my mum bleeding,
Rushing to my room while crying hard,
Falling asleep, I went back to the building.

Lilly-Rose Llewellyn (9)
Bysing Wood Primary School, Faversham

In Space

I was taking off in the rocket and I could hear the engine roaring,
I could see another rocket in the window,
I arrived on the moon, there was another rocket there.

I went to see if there was a person,
Bouncing, I was bouncing everywhere,
I was so happy, there was a person in there,
In the rocket, he's asleep.

Knock, knock, he woke up and opened the door,
He was surprised to see someone,
"Come in!" he said. "Do you want water?"
I said, "No."
We became friends and explored the moon together.
The moon felt soft but it is rock when you fall.

It was so fun on the moon
You can jump everywhere
We decided to go back to Earth
We took off
We were home.

Alfie Pioli (10)
Bysing Wood Primary School, Faversham

The End Of The World

T he disaster strikes.
H orrifying sounds are heard.
E choes of explosions all around.

E normous meteors in the shattered atmosphere.
N o one else is here.
D eath is near.

O n the shaking Earth.
F ire surrounds buildings.

T housands of mutations lurk in the darkness.
H opelessness runs through my veins.
E very nerve tells me to get up.

W aking up in my bed.
O ut of mind thinking I would die.
R ealising it was a dream.
L etting myself, a moment of silence.
D on't worry, it isn't the end of the world.

Harlen Folse (10)
Bysing Wood Primary School, Faversham

Peacefulness

In my dreams, I can see clouds,
all around me and all over the ground.
The moon is singing to me,
the sky is like moving lights.
In the sky it is sparkling,
it is calm and quiet,
I am all by myself, it is peaceful.
Stars in the air, I could walk to them.
There are soft things I am on, rolling in the snuggly
clouds that's what I do.
There is green on the other side,
I am happy.
There is a single tree with a swing, it smells like
perfume and there are flowers surrounding me.
This place is like a beautiful dream.
I went back and I felt calm, it was a mindfulness quiet.

Lily-Grace Wiley (9)
Bysing Wood Primary School, Faversham

In My Dream

In my dreams, I thought it would be a bright time or was it?
Lexi and Evie were behind me
One by one they all came, all of them came, my friends
Suddenly, a black shadow emerged, walking like a zombie
Children's screams grew louder and more prolonged
This shadow just kept coming, not scared of anything
Something creeping moves about
It was creeping around
Our worse fear
Its head was shaped like a stick
It... it... it's a monster... Ahhhh!
Beside it was a clown
Creeping around, we all screamed
Ahhh!
I woke up, thinking it was just a dream...

Ikmat Mayungbe (10)
Bysing Wood Primary School, Faversham

Crossroads

C reeping through my mind, and creeping through my head,
R eally frightened that somebody is under my bed,
O ver in my head somebody said,
S *leep, sleep, sleep, it is just a dream,*
S o I try to, but I just can't,
R ealising that I have a technique,
O n goes my light,
A ll in the dark night,
D one, I'm asleep reading a book peacefully,
S uper happy that I'm calm, but then somebody grabs my arm.

Shakil Boakye Ansah (10)
Bysing Wood Primary School, Faversham

Dancing Alive

As I went into the hall,
There were people at the stall.
I wore my dancing dress,
And shoes as the rest.
But two friends came,
And said, "You look beautiful."
I whispered, "Same, you look beautiful too."
A shadow came behind Tia,
She screamed, "Help!"
With a yelp.
Gone, I was too late, panic, panic,
Everyone was panicking.
Hide, hide under the table,
I grabbed Eliza's hand,
Stick together,
Until the very end.

Shanvi Shandilya (9)
Bysing Wood Primary School, Faversham

The War

W here is everyone? The world is empty
O range is the colour of the sky still filled with smoke
R estaurants run down, lights flickering on and off
L oads of old machinery just sitting there collecting rust
D owntown barricaded off with high walls

W hy did this all happen in the first place?
A ll of this can't be real, can it?
R ealising it was just a dream, I wake up and see the sky filled with smoke.

Toby Brown (10)
Bysing Wood Primary School, Faversham

The Underworld

U nder my feet all I hear are footsteps
N ighttime makes it worse
D on't forget I find a clown more red than red
E than said that we should run
R unning away as fast as we would
W hile the clown still chased like a bear
O ver there we see a road to Earth
R ealising we are hallucinating
L istening to the air and hearing the clown
D ad woke me up realising I had a bad dream.

Dylan Jul-Ellison (10)
Bysing Wood Primary School, Faversham

Builders

Builders dream big,
Big bright bricks,
Without breaking it into bits,
Big walls so high,
That you had to fly.

Glowing in the sky is
A big bright eye,
So far, but so close is a house,
The next step to success.

Brick by brick,
Step by step,
It was finally with a bed,
Flying through my eyes,
I was in the sky.

Woke up so high,
Without the sky,
Just stars with glowing faces.

Max Speed (9)
Bysing Wood Primary School, Faversham

Super Dogs

Dogs flying through the sky.
Trying to find a crime.
Hearing screams, dashing there in despair.
There was nothing there.
Sadly and madly they think to quit.
Quitting is never the answer.
Just think of it.
Sitting there nothing to do.
So boring.
I will become a hero again.
Time to get on to the chase.
Happily catching robbers, saving lives.
Helping people is my life.
It is my thing.

Oscar Pilbeam (9)
Bysing Wood Primary School, Faversham

Superhero

S o it all begins in my house,
U p there is a falling tree,
P eople are very shocked,
E ven as scared as can be,
R ight behind was also a hero,
H e pulled the tree back,
E eek! That's amazing,
R eally not a crack.
O h wow, will there be a hero pack?

Abiola Ogunneye (10)
Bysing Wood Primary School, Faversham

Extinct Dinos

D inos are my dream
I love the king of the dinos
N ow they are extinct
O range, red, green and blue,
S ee now, we only have toys,
A fter the asteroid struck
U nder the darkness
R oaring stopped at once
S adly, they are extinct.

Roman Reeves (10)
Bysing Wood Primary School, Faversham

The Monster

The monster from Friends World
As fluffy as a cloud
Pink like cotton candy
Its moan was very loud
And as tall as a tree
As fat as a rat
Chasing me down the hall
All of a sudden
My brain went rotten
I was on my feet
I ran like a fleet.

Ruby-Lou Adams (10)
Bysing Wood Primary School, Faversham

Travelling Around The World

When you go travelling, you go left, right or forward. Travelling makes you happy, but be careful because there might be some bumps that can even be car crashes that feel painful. The sky is bright and full of light if you are sad or down.

When you go on the plane, you might sleep or be awake for a long time. You might feel happy, sad or scared. Well, not yet. Your ears might get blocked. It is not nice.

When you get to your destination, you might feel happy or excited, whatever you like. You might be there for one day, two days, three days, it might even be for ten days or a week!

It will be fun, so get ready for your adventure.

But my friend, Ivy, got a beautiful flower. It was beautiful and very big, but someone wanted to chop it off and it fell on our car. It was so funny.

Blanka Cichon (7)
Hadley Learning Community - Primary Phase, Hadley

The Ocean Nightmare

T he darkness fell upon the tide.
H iding all you could see.
E verything was gone.

O n the boat, the crew were fishing.
C aptain Aleeza was the boss...
E very fish caught was put in the hold.
A very great white shark swam past the boat.
N ever before had the sailors seen such a big shark!

N ever before had the hungry shark seen so many sailors to eat.
I t was Jaws...
G arishly gigantic.
H umongous was its appetite.
T he sailors were petrified.
M isty waters arose with the tide.
A large fin started to circle the boat.
R aise the sails, we are in trouble.
E xecute or be eaten alive.

Aleeza Arhbab (8)
Hadley Learning Community - Primary Phase, Hadley

Lost In A Dream

One night, I had a dream...
I was sound asleep when I found myself walking in a wood. This woodland was mysterious and breathtaking. Suddenly, an animal jumped out. It was a baby deer. It looked beautiful. A grey coat with cream dots on its back. Then it bounded away into the dark, thick trees.
The leaves swirled around and around. Then it stopped like a blanket covering them once again. For a moment nothing happened. Then I walked a little deeper into the wood. Something moved in the bushes. I walked closer, then a little closer and found a little ball of white. It was a rabbit. I looked into its chocolatey eyes then it spoke and said, "Can you help me and the animals with fighting climate change?"
Then I woke up. I was at home.

Bethany Cocker (8)
Hadley Learning Community - Primary Phase, Hadley

The Dark, Dark Forest...

Once upon a dream in a dark forest...

I am alone... *until* I see a vast monster that is chasing me, shouting in a weird language, like gibberish. He's telling me something is Gelsiebub. *That's his name!* I get it!

But then, he disappears. But then I feel something on my arm. *Argh! Argh! It's a spider and it's eating my arm!* Then, he disappears just like Gelsiebub.

I... I... I feel different. I fling my arm and create a web. I start to swing... I hear a noise so I swing closer and see... a party going on. And, it is full of monsters and spiders so I ask a monster and it is Gelsibub. He says if I want to I could join the party, but I hear a loud noise. It is my mum. After all, it is just a dream.

James Grant (8)
Hadley Learning Community - Primary Phase, Hadley

Moonlight Bunnies!

A bunch of crazy and sometimes lazy bunnies, who like playing in a field of daisies and hopping and skipping around joyfully, come around once every year in the bright moonlight, dancing around and prancing joyfully. It is amazing watching them dancing around. Once, they nearly saw me but I hid in my curtain so they didn't see me. I was eating my tea peacefully. I was looking at the moonlight glow. It was nice but I saw one of the moonlight bunnies appear.

This might sound funny but I love a cute fluffy bunny. I love the way they hop and prance around. They are so quiet. They don't even make a sound.

As they sit under the sparkly moonlit day, it is magical to see, every pleasant year, them dancing and leaping around.

Sienna Bowen (7)
Hadley Learning Community - Primary Phase, Hadley

Flower Power

Up in the sky, there lived a Slip 'n' Slide. He danced and pranced. *Boom!* He saw a golden flower with a wonderful power. *Poof!* Along came a wizard.
"Who are you?"
"I am the most powerful wizard in the world."
"But what you really look like is a piece of gelatine."
"Haha, are you joking?"
"No, I am serious."
A few days later, after night turned into day.
"No, no! Wake up."
"What?"
"The golden flower has lost its power. What should we do?"
"Let's get the pixies."
"Good idea."
The flowers got their powers back.

Katriel Emiantor Itetia (8)
Hadley Learning Community - Primary Phase, Hadley

Beautiful Day

Once upon a time on a lovely day, a beautiful bee came across a beautiful flower kingdom and pollinated all it could.
The bee told all of the worker bees: "Follow me. I will show you a beautiful kingdom," and all of the worker bees pollinated all they could.
But, they couldn't do it all!
The bee and the worker bees went to tell the honeybees: "Follow us!" and the honeybees followed them and the honeybees pollinated all they could.
Then, they went to tell the hive and they all went to the flower kingdom and they pollinated all the beautiful flowers.
What a beautiful day!

Julia Talmacel (7)
Hadley Learning Community - Primary Phase, Hadley

Football!

Playing football is such fun,
Lots of fun for everyone.
Get the ball and score a goal,
Kick the ball to make it roll.
Playing football is such fun,
Lots of fun for everyone.

Play as defence or striker,
Save the goals as a goalkeeper.
Work together, that's the way,
Teamwork helps us when we play.
Play as defence or striker,
Save the goals as a goalkeeper.

Whistles blown by referees,
Time to score some penalties.
Can the keeper make a catch?
Score the goals to win the match.

Dawood Usman (8)
Hadley Learning Community - Primary Phase, Hadley

Bruno The Spy Puppy

Once upon a time, there was a little girl called Lilly. We were best friends. She lived in a cottage. She had beehives. Her bees made honey. We used to have honey on a Sunday. Now we have grown up, we still have honey as a treat for our family. Bees are our future.

Bruno is my very cheeky French bulldog with big, pointy ears and a very droopy face. One day, Bruno went on a secret mission. He had to reach the biggest, blackest and reddest rocket in the universe. He searched for the rocket for days.

Kikeé-Anne Mea (8)
Hadley Learning Community - Primary Phase, Hadley

Bumblebee

Bumblebee, bumblebee,
You are my humble bee,

Buzzing and flying from flower to tree,
Giving us honey, sweet and free,

Bumblebee, bumblebee,
Come to my home and let's have tea,
Then go to a tree,
And meet another bee,
In the warm summer, you are the one I love to see,
Bumblebee, my humble friend,
Let's have a friendship that never ends,
Bumblebee, bumblebee, you are my humble bee.

Naysa Bhatt (8)
Hadley Learning Community - Primary Phase, Hadley

Spiders

A long time ago, there was this girl called Lia. She was afraid of spiders.
One day she went into the woods all alone. She felt scared. Her parents didn't know. She was walking and walking when she saw a giant spider. She ran away. Her parents were looking for her. She didn't know that she was lost but then she finally realised. Her parents found her.
Then she woke up and it was all a dream. Now she is not afraid of spiders anymore.

Kirandeep Swali (8)
Hadley Learning Community - Primary Phase, Hadley

Unicorns Flying To A Rainbow

Here I go in a magical sky
Holding my head up high
Wings are smooth and look shiny
We are flying so highly
To a rainbow filled with colours
Red and yellow, blue and lots of others
Using the colours as a slide
With my mum, we ride and glide
The sun is out and the clouds are fluffy
Suddenly I wake up, it was a dream
I look out the window and smile
I hope I do that again in a while.

Eliza Qasim (7)
Hadley Learning Community - Primary Phase, Hadley

The Stalker

I went all the way to the mountain.
Crash! Bang!
They started to come near me.
I ran back home and told Lilah,
"What's wrong?" said Lilah.
"Two people were running after me," I said.
She said, "Did they hurt ya?"
"Right everyone, lock the door."

Sydah Fathima (7)
Hadley Learning Community - Primary Phase, Hadley

My Mega Adventure

Once upon a time, the sun shone very bright and my adventure would soon say bye-bye. My adventure started with me and my friends all on our feet. My heart started to beat and my feet started to go fast. *Whoosh!* My feet went to beaches, seas, fields... Then I appeared in my normal place and my face gave a big smile.

Bilal T Mumuni Musah (8)
Hadley Learning Community - Primary Phase, Hadley

Hamster

H appy in my home, I snooze all day.
A wake at night, I love to play.
M y name is Padding, I'm brown and fluffy,
S hiny black eyes and a white tummy.
T asty treats I love to nibble,
E very day, I love a cuddle.
R unning around on my wheel.

Carly Galbraith (8)
Hadley Learning Community - Primary Phase, Hadley

Dream World

Dream, dream, what can I see?
Unicorns and dinosaurs chasing me.
What can I see?
A pirate, an astronaut chasing me.
Dream, dream, what can I see?
A magic football coming at me.
I have a nightmare,
Spiders are coming for me,
I wake up and it was all a dream!

Lacey Edge (8)
Hadley Learning Community - Primary Phase, Hadley

The Bee

H ow do bees make honey?
O pen the hive and look inside
N ice sweet honey
E verybody likes it because it's runny
Y ellow and scrummy
B ees are lovely
E verybody is happy
E very bee is black and yellow.

Ivy-Rose Bryant (8)
Hadley Learning Community - Primary Phase, Hadley

Football

I love football, it's the best
I love scoring goals and doing math tests
Scoring from the left, scoring from the right
The crowd are shouting
He is dynamite
Pelé, Best, Ronaldo and Messi
One day I will be remembered
As great as them.

George McDougall (8)
Hadley Learning Community - Primary Phase, Hadley

I Dream About Giraffes

They are long and tall,
In the zoo,
The tallest of them all,
Their necks are long,
They seem so strong,
They eat green leaves,
In my dream, they never sneeze,
If they ever did...

Lily-Mae Smart (7)
Hadley Learning Community - Primary Phase, Hadley

Out Of This World

I was in space and I was in a rocket
I was soaring in the race but it was a little boring in that place
I was nervous but I needed to serve my purpose for the race in space.

Owais Arif (7)
Hadley Learning Community - Primary Phase, Hadley

Once Upon A Scream...

Once upon a scream,
I was in the deep dark woods.
I was a sweet little girl who twirled and slipped,
But one time was different because I tripped!
I landed on a doorstep. I was black and blue,
But there was no one to help me, I needed to move
Out of the way, just in case something big and scary
Came out of the door and kidnapped me.
I was terrified, poor little me.
Then, something came out of the door.
It was furry, like a cat's fluffy fur.
Then, it stared right at me and I stared too,
Then the black thing moved!
Suddenly, I was picked up, I was screaming with fear.
I tried to run but my legs wouldn't work.
I was trapped, terrified and all alone!
I yelled out for help, but nothing was there.
Because the thing covered my mouth, it wouldn't let me scream!
I was taken into the house and I was put on a chair.
Then, I saw what the animal was. It was a big black hare.
Then, the doors were locked. I was stuck in the room.

Then, I heard screaming in my ear and then I woke up.
"It was just a dream. *Phew.*"
Ha, ha, it was just a dream.
I know what I will call it. 'Once Upon A Scream!'
So great and scary, it needed a name.
But what if that did happen? I wouldn't be... *saved!*

Beatrice Hewitt (8)
Hungerford Primary School, Hungerford

I Love Football And Playing With Rubik's Cubes

I , Akshar, won the WC, PL and CL. (Look at the end).

L ove football like me.
O ne person liking football isn't enough.
V ini Jr is really good at football.
E veryone should like...

F ootball!
O h! Ronaldo already plays for Al-Nassr.
O h! Haaland sucks!
T V or football!
B urnley is rubbish.
A kshar is insane in defence.
L ove football.
L ove playing with Rubik's cubes.

Portugal vs Argentina: score – 4-3, I win the WC, Portugal wins.
Chelsea vs Arsenal: score – 7-3, I win the PL, Chelsea wins.
Chelsea vs Juventus: score – 8-6 I win the CL, Chelsea wins again.
S*iu!* I love Ronaldo and Chelsea!

Akshar Patel (8)
Hungerford Primary School, Hungerford

In My Dream, I Could See

A little magical cat who gave me a bat.
I saw it change colour into dynamite sparkles,
Which gave me a shock with a sock.
I was so amazed at what I saw I shook like a silly door.
I said to myself, "Give me a wish or else."
I simply vanished into the wish house,
And was surprised by the sight of a cheeky pink mouse.
I was so amazed at what I saw,
Because I had never seen anything like it before.
I love to say, "Hip hip, hooray!" each and every day.
Next stop was Dynamite Palace,
Where I met a multicoloured dog called Alice.
The magical cat appeared again,
This time with a tutu-wearing wren.
The cat said, "Would you like to go on a trip with us,
On a fire-shooting, flying bus?"

Mia McGowan-Bailey (8)
Hungerford Primary School, Hungerford

Once Upon A Dream...

I woke up in a forest with beautiful trees all around.
Suddenly, I heard a scream.
It was coming from the river.
I rushed over to see.
It was a unicorn.
The unicorn was staring into the river.
She was looking at her reflection.
"Help, help, please. Can you stop me from looking at my reflection?"
"Okay," I said, so I stood in front of her
To block the reflection.
"Thank you for rescuing me."
"You're welcome," I said.
"Now I will grant you one wish," the unicorn said.
"I wish to be your best friend," I said.
The unicorn looked sad.
She had not had a best friend before and I could tell.
"Don't worry. I will teach you."

Elodie Head (8)
Hungerford Primary School, Hungerford

Pegasus Vs Dragon

In my dreams, I can feel: the gushing fountain tickling my feet, the little fish zooming past my toes and the damp grass on my back. It feels soothing.

In my dreams, I can see: a scaly, fierce dragon and a beautiful unicorn with foliage and flowers on its head neighing and growling with terror.

In my dreams, I can smell: the drool of the dragon gushing out of its mouth and the unicorn's power sprinkling on me.

They were battling till dawn but the dragon used his humid, terrifying, nerve-racking flames but the unicorn dodged it!

Then the unicorn used her horn to poke him but he used his tail. *Bang, crash, swoosh.* They weren't on their feet, now they were on their backs.

Ava Cadle (8)
Hungerford Primary School, Hungerford

Magical Mischief Of The Forest

I woke up in a daze,
I realised I had hit my head in a maze,
I jumped up and spun around,
My head was pounding all around,
I saw a whirlpool, I jumped inside,
I found myself in a land of candy,
Where trees were toffee,
Lampposts were candy canes
The grass was green sherbet.

I had a tea party with a fox,
The fox was so small he could fit in a box,
He jumped in the box,
I clambered in after.

I could fit in the box.
How could I fit in?

I went through a portal all shimmering blue,
I arrived back at a place that I recognised,
I was back in my bedroom with no sign of the fox
I lay down to doze, I dreamt about what had happened that day.

Elsie Taylor (8)
Hungerford Primary School, Hungerford

The Jungle Adventure

Once upon a dream
In the jungle, where the creatures were mean
And the spiders were green
And the dragons were by the stream
The fish were so fast they could not be seen

Once upon a dream
In the jungle where the creatures were mean
The bugs were slimy
And the octopi moved funnily

Once upon a dream
In the jungle where the creatures were mean
That's where the monkeys had a king
And the colourful birds did sing

Once upon a dream
In the jungle where the creatures were mean
Where the buffalos danced
The lions pranced
And the tigers happily glanced

Once upon a dream
The creatures were not actually mean!

Jackson Bah (8)
Hungerford Primary School, Hungerford

Nightmares

Once upon a dream, a nightmare comes to life.
Here we go for a scary adventure.
Let's go!
I get to the haunted mansion.
I go in.
I get scared and a little nervous.
I'm with my friend.
I'll be fine.
Spiders crawl up my back.
Skeleton bones crack.
Zombies crunching brains.
After, a zombie bites me in the arm.
I scream.
I get shot by a skeleton.
I turn into a zombie skeleton.
My friend freaks out.
It is time for battle.
The battle goes on for days.
My friend beats me.
The curse is broken.
I am back to normal.
I run for dear life.

I dodge all the arrows.
I'm out, finally.
I wake up.

Ronnie King (8)
Hungerford Primary School, Hungerford

Once Upon A Dream

Roses are red, violets are blue,
This is a poem made just for you.
Me and Bob, the flying robot, were zooming to the deadly pirate ship,
When we got there, we had delicious fish and one chip!
We went to find the golden treasure,
So then I could keep it forever.
I turned around and for a pirate, he was ugly as hell,
So I threw a coin in a well.
The pirate wanted to fight in the night.
So I punched the hairy man's chest,
And started to do my best.
I defeated the pirate and got the treasure,
And ran off with pleasure.
But Bob said, "Can we stay a little bit,
For more fish and one chip?"

Aaron Adam (8)
Hungerford Primary School, Hungerford

The Poem

When I had a kitten
It was ginger
My sister was in the kitchen
And my mum and our neighbour took the kitten
Its name was Anna
Because she loved Anna and Elsa so much
My mum and sister love the kitten
And Elsa and Anna
My favourite kitten was Anna
My mum's was Anna as well
And my sister loved both the kittens
When she bought the kittens
They were scared
So they lay on my mum and sister
On the sofa
This is when we lived in Thatcham
When I was a baby
And my sister was five years old
She was young.

Lillie Smith (8)
Hungerford Primary School, Hungerford

Rugby Player

I am famous and a millionaire

A very good rugby player
M ost best rugby player in the world

T he hardest team I played against
H awks
E vil, they were

B ecause I am so rich
E very person loves me
S ee me play
T hen they love me

A lways, rugby is the best sport
T oday

R ugby is dangerous
U nless you're careful
G et the bad teams
B e proud
Y ou can do it too.

Harvey Thomas (8)
Hungerford Primary School, Hungerford

Cats Walking

C ats were walking like humans
A cat eats rats and they like it
T wo cats saw I was lost, so they helped me
S o I found my parents

W hen I found my parents, they said that I could have some fun!
A nd I found some baby kittens!
L aughed and giggled because it was too cute, they were
K ind to me with the cats and I can play with the kittens
I t was so fun!
N ot to mention, I was hungry, so I ate bats, not rats!
"G oodbye, furry one," I said.

Maria Vacareanu (7)
Hungerford Primary School, Hungerford

My Quest

In a galaxy far, far away
Star Wars!
On the Star Destroyer
I could see a trio of stormtroopers.
So I fought my way through.
Oh no!
One of them shot me!
Luckily, I was wearing Beskar armour because
I'm a Mandalorian
Quickly, I jumped up and grabbed my gun.
But then my friend, Boba Fett, shot the stormtrooper dead!
I saw the room that Grogu was in!
Daringly, I went in.
I struck Moff Gideon down with my Beskar spear!
I'd finished my quest!
Oh no!
It was just a dream!

Frank Smart (8)
Hungerford Primary School, Hungerford

The Dancing Teacher

Once upon a dream
I could see
My teacher dancing with glee
And turning the children into spiders
When eating afternoon tea.
Once upon a dream
I was with
My very best friend
And my seven pets
Eating hot soup.
Once upon a dream
I was
In my red classroom
Shaking with madness.
Once upon a dream
I felt
Scared like a butterfly getting chased
Also confused like a child with no clue.
Then I heard a scream in the hall
But it was just my alarm.

Imogen Giles (7)
Hungerford Primary School, Hungerford

What Happens When Things Come Alive

In my dream,
I looked around my house,
I saw a mouse,
On a woodlouse,
I ran out of my house
To the river,
Saw a duck with a liver,
That same duck had a tight
Top with a light,
I couldn't bear it,
I ran back to my house,
Saw the mouse
On the woodlouse,
I couldn't see much because my eyes were half-closed,
My washing machine had some bows on it and it was farting!
I woke up, nothing was real,
As it was all a dream just like we started.

Caitlin Roff (8)
Hungerford Primary School, Hungerford

A Never-Ending Zoo

Once upon a dream, I woke up in a zoo, and I found my cat sitting beside me. My cat was electric. With my eyes, I could see very, very tall trees. I was frightened. So my electric cat and I tried to find an exit. It was very, very hard to find an exit and my cat and I found an exit but as soon as we found the exit, a very, very big crowd of animals started to surround my cat and me.
My cat and I were so scared until a man came into the zoo and he said, "Shoo, shoo, go away," to the animals.

Indianna Sandell (8)
Hungerford Primary School, Hungerford

Once Upon A Dream

In my dreams, I can see four ponies looking at the treats and sweets.
As I put the treats into the back locker,
They start to put their bottom lip out, what a shocker!

The four ponies, Popcorn, Panda, Rolo and Cloudy,
Are the cheekiest in the county.

I tack them up ready for my friends and I ride on them side saddle.
We canter and trot around the arena like a ballerina.
They were so good I gave the ponies a spa and the treat I hid,
That's what I did.

Olivia Browning (7)
Hungerford Primary School, Hungerford

Lewis And Ronaldo

L ewis likes football
E llie's my cousin
W ill is my friend
I gloos are cold
S he's furry

A pples are yummy
N elly is my sister
D id my work

R abbits are fluffy
O lives are tasty
N onnes, my brother
A my is my second sister
L ollies are crunchy
D ummy likes them
O h no, my dog, I'll be back in one second, come back, please!

Lewis Berry (8)
Hungerford Primary School, Hungerford

Once Upon Pretty Crystals

C rystals are pretty and they are very colourful
R ubies are as red as a beautiful red rose
Y ellow crystals are like sunflowers in a field
S parkling crystals are like diamonds glowing in the moon
T urquoise crystals are like the ocean glistening in the sunlight
A methyst is purple like the purple at evening
L ight-blue crystals are like the sky in daylight
S apphire is blue like the river flowing down the forest.

Isabella Atkins (7)
Hungerford Primary School, Hungerford

Once Upon A Dream...

I woke up in the rainforest with my team.
We were excited for an adventure.
We're going to see lizards and creepy crawlies, I'm sure.

We were walking for a while,
When we saw some crocodiles,
With scary smiles.

They crawled over to us,
And attacked us with their sharp claws,
And gave a horrifying roar.

I awoke with a shock,
To hear a knock!

It was my mummy,
Telling me to get up and hurry!

Cody Lee (8)
Hungerford Primary School, Hungerford

Once Upon A Dream

I was playing with my Xbox in my bedroom
When suddenly I flew into the screen.

I was in Minecraft world where zombies were fighting me
I managed to kill three.

I was playing with my Xbox in my bedroom
When suddenly I flew into the screen.

I was in a speedrun four in Roblox
With doughnuts on the floor.

I was playing with my Xbox in my bedroom
When suddenly I flew into the screen.

Riley Blanchard (8)
Hungerford Primary School, Hungerford

Once Upon A Dream

Once upon a dream, in a world of rhyme
Do you know where you are?
Let's go back in time
Where unicorns graze in graceful meadows
And where dragons are nice, friendly fellows
You live in a castle on a giant hill
With your personal assistant called Robot Jill
Tigers guarding in the woods
They are guarding ghastly goods
Is this a nice, friendly theme?
That's why it's called Once Upon A Dream.

Tommy Taylor (8)
Hungerford Primary School, Hungerford

My Uncle

My uncle has won lots of trophies
He is so good he won't take a low fee
He is one of the best footballers I know
He knows how to make the game flow
My favourite football team is Manchester United
He loves Manchester United too and I know if he was invited
And if my uncle was to play for them
Then my uncle would be their biggest gem
Because my uncle is the best
And I would always be his special guest!

Jamie Greenslade (8)
Hungerford Primary School, Hungerford

Nightmares

N othing has prepared me for this
I don't know where I am
"G o to the left," someone shouts
"H ello," I say. "Hello, what are you doing here?"
T hud! Someone is coming towards me
M illie looks to the left
A hhh!
R un, stop chasing me
E scape, I have to escape
S uddenly, I woke up and turned out to be fine.

Frankie Sprules (8)
Hungerford Primary School, Hungerford

The Wonderful Dream Chocolates

M ars bars are yummy and taste like space
A ero Mints are minty, I personally don't like them
R olos are crunchy and make my mouth water
S nickers are disgusting and make me sick

B irthday cake that is chocolate, yummy, yum, yum
A fter Eights are okay, they taste like a rock cake
R evels are good because they always surprise you!

Gwynnie Binns (8)
Hungerford Primary School, Hungerford

In My Dreams

I could see a penguin eating cake and steak.
I could see a tiger playing chess and making a mess.
I could see a leopard dancing around and making a sound.
I could see a parrot talking and silly walking.
I could see an elephant spinning and crazy swimming.
I could see a giraffe jumping on a float and kicking a boat.
I could see a monkey jumping on a trampoline and his fur was green.

Harrison Martin (7)
Hungerford Primary School, Hungerford

Wizards

I was so happy to get on the train to Hogwarts. I was sorted into Gryffindor. My new life was going to begin. I was so happy to be in my house. I was as happy as a wizard in the sun.
My first lesson was Potions. It was fun.
As it was my last day of my first year, it was the first day of my second year.
Years later, it was the Triwizard Tournament. I put my name in the Goblet of Fire. I was in it.

Ella Baker-Hill (8)
Hungerford Primary School, Hungerford

In My Dreams

In my dreams, I could see a tiger swimming in the woods.
In my dreams, I could see an owl dancing by the canal.
In my dreams, I could see a penguin eating muffin cakes in the jungle.
In my dreams, I could hear red elephants eating crunchy carrots.
In my dreams, I could hear blue lions laughing at the TV.
In my dreams, I could hear purple giraffes singing happy songs.

Luca Westbrook (8)
Hungerford Primary School, Hungerford

In A World Of Rhyme

F ree fleas flew while these fleas flew they
L ooked at cheesy trees because there were only three
Y ou see

A s you can see these fleas are freezing
W hat a horrible day it must have been
A t the moment you see it's freezing even though
Y ou don't understand how hot it usually gets.

Sophie Armstrong (7)
Hungerford Primary School, Hungerford

A Chaotic Jungle

In my dreams, I could see:
A tiger dancing and prancing about.
A penguin in ice skates twirling and swirling in the air, with incredible trance.
In my dreams, I could see:
Baboons playing chess (although the monkey was still the best).
In my dream, I could see:
Me in a giant tree house, the hustle begins to end and the peace is restored.

Zoë Potolo-Rees (8)
Hungerford Primary School, Hungerford

Once Upon A Dream

Near a stream, there was a poor man,
Who didn't have any jam!

Aliens moved right outside his house.

I helped him with inventions, big and scary.
It was daring alright, I nearly went home early!

So I went outside to greet the aliens, but before I could,
They all shouted, "Cheese and peas, please!"

Jackson Southwell (8)
Hungerford Primary School, Hungerford

Planet Caddy

P lesiosaurus swimming
L and far away
A s I cuddle koalas
N ow it is time to sweep
E arly
T he leap is as deep as a pool

C andy is everywhere
A s I eat it, it fizzes
D emocracy is hot
D eterminedly, I got what I wanted
Y apping loudly.

Norbet Kroker (8)
Hungerford Primary School, Hungerford

Once Upon A Dream

Once upon a dream,
I saw something very mean,
It was very big and scary,
And also very hairy.

Once upon a dream,
I saw something very mean,
It was very happy,
And it was wearing a nappy.

Once upon a dream,
I saw something very mean,
It had a yellow mane,
Which looked like a flame.

Bailey Charman (7)
Hungerford Primary School, Hungerford

Not Giving Up

Miles away from my house
It doesn't matter if it shines so bright
Leading my way home, wolves so jolly in my heart
When I arrive, bright colours block my way
While resting, I gaze in fascination
Finally, I find my way
Bursting with happy tears
Stroking my pets
My love for them will always go on.

Amber Duca (8)
Hungerford Primary School, Hungerford

Untitled

Scary, hairy spider,
Sitting in his cobweb house,
Pretty hairy spider,
With long eyelashes,
Icy cold cobwebs all around,
Dangerous with superpowers,
Shooting icy cobwebs,
An enormous spider is protecting our house,
Run, run, spiders, go back home,
Sneaky spiders creep back home.

Henry Ellis (7)
Hungerford Primary School, Hungerford

Dragon

D reams are crazy, I had one about a dragon
R euben the dragon lived in a mansion
A Reese's Pieces mansion
"**G** reat," Reuben said, "do you want to come in?"
"**O** h, yes please." We ate chocolate all day
N o, it was a dream.

Ted Thatcher (7)
Hungerford Primary School, Hungerford

Angel, My Pet

A ngel's nickname is Amazing Apple!
N elly is her BFF
G arden for fresh air
E llie is her cousin
L ions are her favourite animal

P ineapples are yellow
E yes shine bright
T eddies at night and science this afternoon.

Hermione Allard (8)
Hungerford Primary School, Hungerford

Once Upon A Dream, Or Is It A Dream?

In my dream, I could see my furry unicorn eating some hay.
In my dream, I wanted to go on my unicorn and ride as fast as a cheetah.
In my dream, I rode my unicorn and felt so sick that I turned green,
It wasn't a dream...
I woke up and I was pedalling on my golden, sparkly bike.

Louanna Annetts (8)
Hungerford Primary School, Hungerford

Candyland

Far away is Candyland
Where it snows ice cream
And the lakes and rivers rain chocolate
And my house is made out of gum
And the ground is made of jelly beans
And the jellybean rides are at the end
You fall into jelly beans
And I'm with my best friend Lewis.

Will Cassidy (8)
Hungerford Primary School, Hungerford

Dragon Attack

D ark eyes flashing like fireballs in the night,
R ed wings dazzling in the distance,
A mazing claws as sharp as a bird's beak,
G orgeous teeth shining with hunger,
O utrageously long pointy tail
N orbert is his name.

Millie Taylor (8)
Hungerford Primary School, Hungerford

Cats And Dogs

C ute
A s a
T eddy's
S mooth fur

A nd being touched
N icely
D efinitely

D reamy
O verpoweringly
G orgeous
S oft dogs and cats.

Aria Armstrong (8)
Hungerford Primary School, Hungerford

Jaguars

J aguars are big cats, they are scary
A nxious about what to eat
G asping at the antelope
U nbroken concentration
A s he is about to pounce
R *oar!* A lion made the antelope run away.

William Fisher (8)
Hungerford Primary School, Hungerford

Sweets

S prinkles make my mouth water
W hat a lovely taste
E ating sweets is amazing
E clairs taste disgusting
T wix sounds as weird as ever could be
S weets are amazing, I eat them every day.

Ava Kirby (7)
Hungerford Primary School, Hungerford

Vicario

V ictorious goalkeeping
I n a stadium
C ould I save all the goals?
A ll the fans were happy
R unning on the pitch
I t was so easy to do
O ur team got a penalty.

Oscar Hall (8)
Hungerford Primary School, Hungerford

Spiders

I am alone, spiders surround me,
I am scared as a wild bird, jumping!
In front of me, spiders keep surrounding me,
I feel a tingle, I'm growing black legs,
I am a *spider!*

Oliver Day (8)
Hungerford Primary School, Hungerford

Dragons

D ecades ago
R ainforest
A shape wrapped my legs
G o away
O n my way home
N o more adventures
S leep.

Nicole Buck (8)
Hungerford Primary School, Hungerford

Nightmare

A haiku

The king of the sky,
I torture people at night,
While they are sleeping!

Jaxon Pavier (8)
Hungerford Primary School, Hungerford

Spider

Scary, hairy spider sitting
In his cobweb house
Pretty, hairy spider
Cobwebs all around
Run, run, spider - *go back home!*

Arya Little (7)
Hungerford Primary School, Hungerford

Jax

J oyful
A nd
e **X** hilarating.

That is me!

Jax Haines (8)
Hungerford Primary School, Hungerford

Unicorn Dream

Dancing on rainbows, I fall asleep in my bed
But I wake in the clouds, they look like cotton candy,
could it really be?

I look around and see
A colourful rainbow next to me!
I see a pot of shiny gold
So I climb up to retrieve it.

But on the top, there are pink fluffy unicorns
Dancing on rainbows
So I run over to join in
We boogie, we woogie.

Come and join the unicorn conga
And my favourite all-time
The unicorn floss!

I tell the unicorns,
My plan is to get the sparkling gold
They say to fly down the rainbow,
So that is what we will do.

We go to the rainbow
But I realise it's just a dream
I sigh, I guess I'll have to face reality again.

China-Rose Henry (10)
Killisick Junior School, Arnold

Dream Town

I leaned out of the window,
A cool breeze flew across my face,
As the planets pace.

The moon was dreaming,
The stars were gleaming,
But the sun was beaming.

I dreamed of driving on an empty road,
The speed lightening my load,
As I took twirls and whirls.

Welcome to Dream Town,
Where the suns never go down,
Our moon wears the light like a gown,
You can't possibly hold a frown.

Once you've been, you hold much joy,
But you realise it's more of a toy,
No nightmares in Dream Town,
All the nightmares go down.

Georgia Poyzer-Green (10)
Killisick Junior School, Arnold

My Little Imagination

I always imagined
To be a footballer
But sometimes I wished I was a little bit taller.

The graceful little stars light up in the sky
So when I'm high
Finally, I will reach the sky.

When I'm taller and older
I want to be the next Yamal
The greatest player
To kick the ball.

I want to be tall
I want to be the best
Better than the rest.

I always imagine
To be a footballer
But, now I know
I'm now a little bit taller.

Oheneba Opoku (10)
Killisick Junior School, Arnold

The Glee Of Nature

The owls twit,
The waves hit,
And still not a word to be found.

The gate swung open,
The bushes swept past,
While the bin went *bang!*

Blossom drops,
While bunnies hop,
On a hot day.

The busy oak tree,
Smiles happily,
While birds fly with glee.

You see nature is glee,
So come with me,
Then you will see.

We can explore the world,
It will be fun,
Then you will see all of my glee.

Yes, nature is glee,
And if you don't see it,
Come with me.

Grace Fearnley (10)
Killisick Junior School, Arnold

The Horse In My Dreams

Every night
In my dreams
I see a horse
In pure white.

It gallops smoothly
Its mane is like glass
Hooves like brass.

It offers me a ride
Each and
Every night.

I kindly accept
Showing respect.

We gallop over mountains and lakes
It gallops confidently
Showing no mistake.

Suddenly
I trip and fall
The creature disappears.

I wake up alone
In my bed.

The ride was
Just a dream.
Beatrice Ho (9)
Killisick Junior School, Arnold

It Is Night-Time

I look outside through the window
To see freckles of starlight.

The radiant moon
Gossips happily with the stars
And it becomes night-time.

The colossal car
Comes drifting down the road
As fast as a cheetah.

The little scraps
From the dustbin
Scatter everywhere and litter.

Helplessly,
The scared dog scampered past the alleyways.

The timid hedgehog snuffles slowly with the running leaves.

Joanna Onyeso (10)
Killisick Junior School, Arnold

Moon And Stars

I'm flying up to the moon,
Wishing that I'll get there soon.
Swishing and swirling like a balloon,
I love the moon.

Shining bright like a star,
It never feels like I'm too far.
My face was as red as Mars,
I love the stars.

The moon and stars are like my best friends,
When I dream of them my imagination never ends.
Constellations I love to see,
Glittering and shining all around me.

Atia Morrell (9)
Killisick Junior School, Arnold

The Galaxy Above

Cheerfully
The moon hugs the gloomy dull planets.

The glaring bulged window
Shows the moon his reflection and he shines.

Astonishingly
The amazing Milky Way
Rotates, making smiles.

Cautiously
Sleek creatures creep around
Sniffing for food.

Bright hotels
Ascend effortlessly
They are as tall as the stars.

Wind
Swiftly soars around the town.

Kennedy Mason (10)
Killisick Junior School, Arnold

Midnight Magic

At midnight,
The dazzling moonlight shines
Through my window.

A young fox slyly
Hunts for prey as
Its hunger grows.

At an alleyway,
A lone car accelerates
Down a long alleyway.

Dramatically,
Many stars shine brightly
While they prance around the moon.

As the sun rises,
I ask a question,
"Dare shall I enter?"

Lu Chen (10)
Killisick Junior School, Arnold

My Little, Little Teddy Bear

Little, little teddy bear,
I feel that you're
Really alive.

Little, little teddy bear,
I like your
Cute, small eyes.

Little, little teddy bear,
Your eyes are
Shining like
Diamonds in the dark.

Little, little teddy bear,
You are the best
Friend in the
Whole world,
That is why I
Always like you.

Cherish Chan (10)
Killisick Junior School, Arnold

Manchester City

Phil Foden is the most talented kid in the world.
He is part of a dream trio
With Kyle Walker and Jack Grealish.
Foden scores some worldies,
Phil Foden has the most skills.
He can do through balls,
He can score tap-ins,
He can score worldies
And he has a beautiful cross.
Even though he is young,
He still has a beautiful future ahead of him.

Kian Scott (10)
Killisick Junior School, Arnold

The Darkness

I scout out through the curtains,
Dreamily admiring the awe-inspiring night.

The dusty moon,
Is alone with this sparkling sun.

The dazzling streetlight,
Glows brightly,
As the luminous stars twinkle beautifully above.

The cunning fox,
Sneaks hungrily.

The dazzling birds,
Glide gracefully.

Jemima Onyeso (10)
Killisick Junior School, Arnold

The Pink Rose

In summer, the pink rose blooms
Making its visitors smile.

In autumn, the pink rose petals fall
Bringing happiness and joy.

In winter, the pink rose is hidden
In the snow.

In spring, the pink rose will come again
Followed by the warm weather.

Lois Camfield (9)
Killisick Junior School, Arnold

Space Above

The expensive window,
Closes tightly.

Magically,
The dazzling moon floats.

The sleepy hedgehog,
Snuffles.

The twirling curtains,
Sparkle magically.

Magically,
The cars sparkle dazzlingly.

Cain Morrison (10)
Killisick Junior School, Arnold

Sweet Dreams

Once upon a dream
Where the silver light goes
Nobody really knows
Dancing through the stars and moon
Your imagination is the colour of your dream
Sleep tight, my baby,
Enjoy your adventure
Till we see the morning sun again.

Khloe Mitchell (9)
Killisick Junior School, Arnold

Monster And Dragon

My monster:
My monster has large red eyes,
He has sharp pointed teeth,
He has slimy, sludgy skin.

My dragon:
My dragon has eyes as round as dinner plates,
It has sharp teeth to catch its prey.

Oliver Wilkinson (10)
Killisick Junior School, Arnold

The Space

When I look
Up in the sky
I see the moon

And beautiful
Stars, the sky
Looks so beautiful

I just wonder
What it looks like in
Space because
It's so beautiful.

Jeremiah Onyeso (10)
Killisick Junior School, Arnold

Euphoria Unleashed: The Ode To Football's Glory

In a realm where dreams take flight,
Where emotions soar amidst the fight,
A saga unfolds, both fierce and true,
As I bring to you a table of soccer's hue.

Blessed Chipandambira (10)
Killisick Junior School, Arnold

The Eight-Headed Sabretooth

I was once flying by,
Until I heard someone cry.
I flew down
And I saw him drown.
So I asked him, "How did you drown?"
He said, "I was walking by until I fell down."
I said, "Are you okay?"
He said, "Yes, I'm fine, but I have a quest for you.
You must fight the eight-headed sabretooth.
You can pick a pet too, he always likes you."
We flew by and glided into the sky,
Until we heard a loud roar so we decided to hide.
We searched everywhere to check it was clear,
Until we heard a loud stab and we saw a spear.
We walked by and had a big bump
And that's when we saw it, the eight-headed sabretooth.
I felt like it was taking my soul,
My worst nightmare, I could barely fall.
When I got dead,
I woke up safe in bed.

Arlind Kullaj (9)
Lakenham Primary School, Norwich

Space Axolotls

Galaxies for gills,
Stardust for skin,
Planets for eyes,
Meteors firing from their mouths.
Roaming through the multiverse.
I wake up confused,
I'm riding on a space axolotl.
Its skin is silky smooth.
It fires out a meteor which destroys the moon.
Gulping up the remains,
The babies come to feast.
And I want to try too.
So nervously, I jump onto a baby.
Startled, it looks around frantically,
So I try to calm it down,
And my pockets have some moon in.
I softly bite into it.
It tastes of cheese!
I split it with the baby.
It instantly calms down.
But now, I am safe at home.
One moment, I was out there.
Next, I was here.

I look in my pockets
And they are filled with moon.

Freddie Seal-Coon (9)
Lakenham Primary School, Norwich

Moon Dragons

I see a dragon flying in the air
Its beauty makes me forget my cares
Its blue wings, yellow tail and its magenta eyes,
Glittering in the moonlit sky.
I would like to ride on her back,
When the sky is really black.
I will see the queen behind the scenes,
And hope to always have dragons in my dreams.
I have lots of dreams, unicorns, monsters,
But I love dragons when they soar through the sky,
Like clouds blown by the wind.
I will always love dragons!

Dali Cooper (9)
Lakenham Primary School, Norwich

Arachnids

A dream I hated came to me again
R ight when I was deep asleep in my bed
A nd then my worst fear appeared
C racking and crumbling eggs began to hatch
"H elp!" I shouted but no one could hear
N ewborn creatures doubling every second
I wanted to run but my legs didn't move
D evilish eyes stared into my soul
S piders in my bed, my house, my nightmare!

Noah McCloy (8)
Lakenham Primary School, Norwich

Out Of This Dream

In this dream, I have tonight,
I wake up below colour and bright,
I get up feeling like it's noon,
Oh no, I'm on the moon,
I take my first step, flying in the air, thinking,
I have no time to spare,
As I rush to get out of here,
I fall into a crater with a face full of fear,
As my head is about to land on the bottom,
I wake up in bed, realising there's no problem.

Charlie King (9)
Lakenham Primary School, Norwich

Moonbeam The Sky Dancer

U nique, exquisite mane with locks of salmon-pink and red.
N ever dull nor dark, just rainbows within.
I vory-white spiralled horn, expressing happiness and joy.
C olourful hooves with all the moves.
O paque crystals and moonbeam stars.
R ainbow colours, red, pink, purple, green and blue.
N o such thing as a dreary unicorn!

Sophia Chapman (9)
Lakenham Primary School, Norwich

Wizard's Light

Wizard's light, shines very bright
It's time to shine
Don't be a fright, you have to listen well then
You will make a right and make a light bright
In the night,
Now you have to make a kite light up
Put the fright in the light, there is no being scared tonight
I told you it's alright, never be afraid to lose.

Lola-Mae Smith (9)
Lakenham Primary School, Norwich

A Lovely Dancer (A Friend)

Every night, she is dancing in the hall,
She is the brightest star of all.
Every day, her and I dance into a delightful trance,
It's just like waving a magic wand in the sky.
This is something truly that money just can't buy,
A friendship through dancing for her and I.

Mollie Molloy (8)
Lakenham Primary School, Norwich

Football

I enjoy playing football in a team.
To play with Ronaldo is my dream.
To suddenly be praised.
My friends and my family are amazed.
With my super fast boot.
I came to shoot.
"Goal!" they shouted as the ball went in
And then it hit the bin.

Cameron Bamber (9)
Lakenham Primary School, Norwich

The Candy Land

It's the sweetest land,
The colourful popcorn trees grow,
The gummy flowers pose,
The candyfloss is very happy,
The candy village is happy,
It's very fun,
You can explore lots of things,
I wish I could go there,
It's the best.

Nanthitha Lenin (9)
Lakenham Primary School, Norwich

The Tormented Ghosts

Pale ghosts creep,
Spirits wail in sorrow,
Unforgiving souls howl to avenge their untimely deaths,
The old shrieking shack bathed in moonlight,
A silent garden remembers nothing,
I wake up with sweat on my brow.

Eleanor Quinlan (9)
Lakenham Primary School, Norwich

Dragons And Unicorns

D uring the night in my deepest slumber
R ealising I was in a magical land
A nd then I saw a mythical creature
G iant, fierce-looking, scary beast
O verhearing him was a horse like, "Ooo!"
N eighing ferociously
S oon after, I looked at them

A nd this is what they said, "We need you."
N ow, this place was being attacked
D irectly looking at me!

U nderstandably, I said, "Okay."
"N ow then," said the dragon, "hop on me."
I was afraid I'd fall off, but I didn't
C autiously, I got off and we were there
O n the battlefield, there were black and
R ed magic spells being cast
N ow it was battle time, the dragon used its fire-
breathing and everything was a blur!
S o, I wish I could tell you more, but for now, bye!

Zakaria Shah (9)
Stechford Primary School, Birmingham

I've Got Superpowers

Once upon a dream, I was flying on top of the clouds. Then a flying horse came and said to me, "Take these shields, they have superpowers."
Then I took them, and I said, "What do I need to do with these superpowers?"
The horse said, "You need to fight the dragon called Tommy." The horse said, "The dragon is here now. You need to fight for victory."
I said, "I can't fight alone. Maybe you and I both can fight?"
Then the horse said, "You've got the powers, use them."
So I did use the shield which had powers, and the dragon was roaring. Fire was coming out of his mouth and stamping here and there. Then the dragon fell down. The powers I had were really strong powers. Then the horse got happy, and we became friends, and I gave the Superpower Shield back to the horse.

Mohammad Zain (9)
Stechford Primary School, Birmingham

Flowers

F lowers are so bright, they look like a light,
L ovely and cute, sparkles on them too,
O n the hill with the plants
W ith spiders, flies and ants,
E ven with bees sucking up pollen to make honey,
R aindrops falling bit by bit on the cute bunny
S oil on it, to make it grow bigger and bigger.

They are placed so neatly,
They are giving all of the beauty,
And grow when I get old.
They grow so lovely and great
Butterflies flying around with their mate
Flowers are the best, you should get some rest,
They give you a flow, but you're always staying still,
Flowers need some air, but they don't have hair.

Falak Kamran (9)
Stechford Primary School, Birmingham

The Supreme Dream

One night
In my dream
I woke up
And felt supreme
Why am I supreme?
You may ask
Because I found an amazing wand
A spell it could cast
But it couldn't cast a thing
That was a puzzle to me
It was plain old boring
Nothing magical I could see
At that moment
A witch came to my door
But I wasn't interested
Staring with bore
"Give it boy!"
She said with no glee
I shouted out
"How'd you know I'm a he?"
"Just give me the wand,"
She said with sadness

I said, "Okay!
Hold your madness!"
But she didn't listen
And kept screaming
I woke from my dream
No witch, no wand
But I still feel supreme.

Muhammad Musa Umer Binyameen (9)
Stechford Primary School, Birmingham

The Creepy Forest

Once there was a girl lost in a creepy, scary forest.
She was always scared when mice would eat her rice.
One day, there was an enormous spider with a horse rider.
She was screaming for help but no one would dare to help.
Until one day, a friendly lady came to help her.
Because she had been before.
The lady stood in front of the girl,
The girl stood up and gave her a hug.
The lady asked her if her name was Emma.
The girl said, "Yes."
Emma asked how she knew her name.
She took her hood off and it was her older sister.
She asked how she knew where she was.
Her older sister explained.
Soon, they were both lost.
So Emma made a suggestion...

Aizah Fatima (8)
Stechford Primary School, Birmingham

The Dreams Of An App

I slept like I was in a current,
And I dreamt and dreamt,
About something like a map,
It looked like it was made of scrap.
I recognised I was an app,
I had a big, red scab,
Then I found out I was YouTube,
And then I was shaped as a cube.
Then I began to cry,
I felt like I was going to die,
I thought there was a cure,
It had to be pure.
Whenever people pressed me,
I felt like I was burnt tea.
I thought it wasn't that bad,
Little did I know I was about to go mad.
But after a while, it wasn't that bad,
I wasn't that sad about being mad,
And in fact, I was happy,
And I definitely never felt like a nappy.

Anayah Alam (9)
Stechford Primary School, Birmingham

David Attenborough

D own in the Serengeti,
A man you might find,
V ideoing the animals,
I nspiring generations,
D iscovering new species.

A nimals need our protection,
T heir habitats are being destroyed,
T hey are part of our world too,
E ven though he is...
N inety-eight years old,
B elieving we can make a difference,
O ffering nature a place in our world,
R ealising the damage we are doing,
O n and on he travels,
U ntil everyone hears the message,
G enerations should follow his example,
H e is a great man.

Daniel Vaughan (8)
Stechford Primary School, Birmingham

Part One: We Are Here

I am on a mission to picture the dinosaurs. Some are herbivores and some are carnivores. No matter what shape or size; some are small, some are big and some are medium. Oh, and I forgot, there are some dinosaurs that are omnivores. It means they eat meat and plants.
The adventure begins right here. Argh, we're here again.
"What's the mission, boss?"
"The mission is to picture a dinosaur. No matter what, you've got to picture them. Understand?"
"Yep, understood, boss."
"Good luck!"
"But what..."
"Shhh! Great, now picture it."
"Let's go and find them!"

Aariz Bin Haroon (9)
Stechford Primary School, Birmingham

The Magic Adventure

There once was a girl called Ruqayyah. She was nine years old, she loved kittens.
Suddenly, there was an earthquake and a portal opened. It was purple and Ruqayyah wanted to explore, so she went through the portal and was surprised to see rainbows everywhere and soft cotton clouds.
Ruqayyah was so eager to walk and that's what she did. She saw a unicorn, it had a colourful horn and brown fur. She wanted to touch it but if she did she would get splinters in her hand and she was so amazed about what she had seen so far and she liked this adventure so much. She even thought it was magical and now it was time to go. Bye for now.

Ruqayyah Hussain (9)
Stechford Primary School, Birmingham

Smiley Face Land

In my dreams every night
I see smiley faces that give me a fright
They all just jump around
But one was by the lake and it drowned
One time they were racing
But one smiley was just chasing
They were doing something that was creepy
But made me rather sleepy
I lay down and had a little sleep
But I woke up from a sound that was *beep*
I woke up to see that the beep
That sounded like a jeep
Was from my school alarm
Which I wish I had put under a bomb
I sat up in my bed
And for some reason, it smelt like something was dead.

Rumaisa Ansar (9)
Stechford Primary School, Birmingham

Superpowers

I have powers, look and see,
Over there is a tree.
Can you watch and see,
Until I make it fly to me?
Can you see that tiny bee?
Watch it come as I turn it into a flea.
Over there, under the tree,
Can you see the kitty all alone?
What a pity!
Watch as I make its mother appear.
Look how happy it is to see its mother's face with no fear.
My powers are strong,
They don't all of a sudden go wrong.
I have strong powers, so I don't need help.
I've got good at my powers now.

Aleeza Arzu (9)
Stechford Primary School, Birmingham

A Good Dream

A good dream,
Has a good beam,
That lights up every star at night,
That catches everyone's sight,
With all my friends,
'Til the night ends,
We look up to the stars,
And say how bright they are!
Lying down time by time,
"Look at the sun shine!"
Laughing together like we are sisters,
All of a sudden I hear a voice,
"Wake up, time for school!"
Oh well, it was just a good drool!

Yasmina Hashemi (8)
Stechford Primary School, Birmingham

Dream House

D arkness as light can be,
R efurbishing is the key,
E avesdropping is easy,
A round are neighbours that are friendly,
M elodies that it sings to me.

"H ello," they say,
O h I am so gay,
U m let me cry in happiness if I may,
S ince day one I have been feeling the sun rays,
E veryone wants to stay in this house for the rest of their days.

Zorian Khan (9)
Stechford Primary School, Birmingham

Dreamland

What would it be without you, my tree?
A vision without my friend
Or a summery day
Or a portal to Mars, what shall it be?
So hop into the portal to Mars
And you will be there
Hear the moaning
Come on now, have a water fight
Dream, dream, dream
All is there
So eat whatever
All you need is a summery day
So shout out and say, "*Dreamland!*
Here we come."

Haleema Ahmad (9)
Stechford Primary School, Birmingham

The Dinosaur

I was walking down the street,
When I saw a dinosaur at my feet.
I felt the need to try and retreat,
But I felt the need to try another treat.
But it looked up at me with its shiny teeth,
He tried to bite me but I dodged his shiny teeth.
I ran and he was far from me,
But there was a dinosaur in front of me.
So I screamed, "I need to run or I will be a feast!"

Muhammad Ukasha Ali (9)
Stechford Primary School, Birmingham

Teacher

The reason why I chose this idea is because all teachers are nice, helpful and the best teachers. This is for my other teachers and also for my teacher.
My dream is to be a teacher. I dreamt about being a teacher and other jobs whatsoever.
My teachers are my idols because they have been helping me since Reception until now.

Ali Awan (9)
Stechford Primary School, Birmingham

Flying Gorillas

I just woke up and I fell into a portal. I was by myself. I was so confused. Where was I right now?
I saw a gorilla flying. I was looking for my family members. Were they here? No, they were not. Now I was scared that I might pee myself.
Then I saw a whole army of gorillas flying. Then I saw that I was on Jupiter!

Adam Hussain (9)
Stechford Primary School, Birmingham

Once Upon A Dream

In my dream every night birds fly round the rainbow and the rainbow shines, sparkling in the sky. And one by one eagles go flying and twirling around the rainbow, making beautiful signs. And the eagle hears sounds above the roofs and hears the shooting stars shooting towards the eagles.

Divine Djala (9)
Stechford Primary School, Birmingham

Monster

I'm walking on the shore,
But then I hear a roar,
I see a monster,
Who is a boxer,
Who is chasing me,
Before it sits under a tree,
Which then it falls asleep.

Isa Hussain (9)
Stechford Primary School, Birmingham

My Mum Is Amazing

My mum is amazing
She looks after me
She is so sweet just like honey
Everyone's mum is special
But my mum is one of a kind.

Saima Rehman (9)
Stechford Primary School, Birmingham

Pop Star Dream

P eeking in my dreams every night,
O n stage a teenage girl with a wig on tight,
P op star girl trying to live a normal life,

S inging on stage, everyone wants to be her wife,
T he life everybody wants, driving in a nice car.
A nd I'm the one who wants a normal life, but also be a pop star,
R iding on a horse with me but also singing with the pop star, with me as well.

D ancing in the crowd, everybody will be so old and yell.
R ushing on the stage whilst I'm shining big.
E verybody will dig just to see,
A sparkly stage just for me,
M e now waking up to realise what I want to be!

Minnie Hamilton (9)
Sutton Manor Community Primary School, Sutton Manor

The Gingerbread House

Once upon a time, in the land of sweets,
I could smell a yummy cake,
I said to myself, "I think it is freshly baked."
In the distance, I saw a cat,
She looked sad, but she was chasing a rat,
The cat was not very bright,
"I am going to call you 'Moonlight'.
Hey! Moonlight, don't hurt that rat, it is mean!
Moonlight, look, a house made of gingerbread and jelly bean.
It smells delicious, I am very keen. Remember not to hurt the rats, don't be mean.
Wow, there is a blanket made out of candy, it is delicious.
Oh that is the rat, Moonlight, don't be vicious."

Esmé Wright (9)
Sutton Manor Community Primary School, Sutton Manor

The Night, Strangest Of My Life

Last night, I was sleeping in my bed,
Then my face turned red.
I jumped out of my bed,
Then saw an elephant dancing on my bed.
I went outside and saw a swimming bed,
It had a deathly growl.
I saw a flying tree,
Then I said, "It's not for me,"
And the tree fell to its death.
I went back home and saw something on the road,
It must have been a toad.
I saw a mat mooing in my house,
I heard something, it was a wizard.
I saw Zeus,
And then I saw a big Boost.

Billy Sutton (8)
Sutton Manor Community Primary School, Sutton Manor

Meeting My Friend

Once upon a time, I went to the zoo and saw an animal that was hairy.
So then I went to my garden and I saw a fairy.
In my dreams, I got a letter saying I could go to tea,
And I was so excited, I was going to wee.

When the moon and the stars started to shine,
I wrote a letter to my friend to come and play with me.
So I tossed the letter in a bottle of sprinkles from a potion,
Then I went to the beach to send my letter to my friend,
And I decided to put it in the ocean.

Phoebe Langley (8)
Sutton Manor Community Primary School, Sutton Manor

Making A Friend

At night, crazy things enter my head,
And I am woken by a huge dragon, scaly and red.

"Hello," says the dragon. "Bob is my name.
And finding a friend is the reason I came."

Me and Bob go to the forest but weirdly everything is blue,
We search up and down, trying to find a clue.

Then suddenly I get superpowers that make me glow.
I turn to Bob and say, "Off we go."
I go to the cinema and there's a person with a broken toe.

George Mellor (8)
Sutton Manor Community Primary School, Sutton Manor

The Nightmares

Every night I see a park,
I bang my head, oh a spark!

Why am I in a big wood?
I am now in a pile of mud!

I look up and see a clown,
Uh oh, I see a big frown.

I quickly run far, far away,
I get home and there I will stay.

Suddenly, I wake up in bed,
My face turns a bright red.

I run to my old mum,
Oh god, I am done!

She asks me what's wrong,
I decide to sing a long song.

Esmee Dyer (9)
Sutton Manor Community Primary School, Sutton Manor

Fairy Land

In my dreams every night,
I imagine Fairy Land with clouds as bright,
Tree houses up so tall,
And they are round, like a ball.
The fairies and I fly through the woods,
And we go to the floor,
The fairies' wings shine so bright,
In the dark, bright moonlight night.
Sometimes I feel alone without my fairy friends every day,
That's why I love my bed,
When I wake up every day, my hair turns red.

Hayley (9)
Sutton Manor Community Primary School, Sutton Manor

The Mad Circus

Last night I was sleeping in my bed,
Suddenly, my face turned red,
I was scared,
Because of the bird.
Then the birds came to me,
And they longed to be a bee.

Then the bee stung the bird,
Then I heard the birds chirping outside the lair.

The blinds were annoying,
And I was boiling.

Then I ran away to an upside-down world,
And there was a hound.

Oliver Craig (9)
Sutton Manor Community Primary School, Sutton Manor

Clown Murder

Last night I was sleeping in my bed,
And my face turned red.
Once upon a time, I was in this giant balloon,
And it fell down and made a big pop.
Once upon a time, I was walking in my door,
I noticed that I was poor,
So I was freezing and next I lived on the streets now.
I jumped out of my bed, startled and scared,
Because I saw a clown and I screamed the full house down.

Lexi Atherton (9)
Sutton Manor Community Primary School, Sutton Manor

The Horror Clown

Last night, I was sleeping in my bed,
And suddenly my face started to go red.
A scary clown entered my mind,
He was definitely not the friendly kind,
He had a very scary frown,
And I felt like it was a horror clown.
I ran away as fast as I could,
And felt like I smelt a load of blood.
I felt like I was in full of dread,
And suddenly I found myself in my bed.

Athisha Kopinath (9)
Sutton Manor Community Primary School, Sutton Manor

The Long Adventure

In a mansion big and old,
The room felt cold.

Then my husky found a huge, ancient door,
It looked like it came out of the war.
I entered and I saw all of my friends in the sky,
I was happy, crying,
I woke up in my bed,
It was velvet red.
My black and white cat,
It was on my mat,
My husky licked me just in time,
And I travelled back in time.

Sofie Veseia (9)
Sutton Manor Community Primary School, Sutton Manor

The Elephant

Last night I was sleeping in my bed,
I suddenly saw someone dead.

I jumped out of my bed because there was a murder,
Then I got bit by a monster named Purder.

I went to the window to have a large burp,
I then saw a phone talking to an elephant.

I woke up out of bed and I saw an elephant on my bed,
Its skin was not grey it was red.

Marley Kelsall (9)
Sutton Manor Community Primary School, Sutton Manor

The Dream Of Candy

In a land of sweets and candy,
It's marshmallows that's handy.

In the magical land, I found a map,
But ended up in a trap.

There's a toffee hut,
With a giant purple foot.

Suddenly, I end up in my bed,
Then my face is turning red.

It's the end,
Ready to send.

Elliot Kovac (9)
Sutton Manor Community Primary School, Sutton Manor

The Unfriendly Clown

One night, I was walking in the wood,
Someone was watching me, I could smell blood,
I felt like there was an unfriendly clown,
I looked behind, he had a scary frown.
I ran away as fast as I can,
And felt like I was as hot as a boiling pan.
I felt like I was full of dread,
And found myself in bed.

Mia Mohamed (9)
Sutton Manor Community Primary School, Sutton Manor

Odd Islands

In a strange land far away,
People still shoot with bows today,
And in this land, monkeys are king,
And humans are slower, controlled by a king,
Thousands of people go and flock,
To try to put these people in a lock,
But one day, a person found a bee,
Which is also holding a tree.

Rowan Fletcher (9)
Sutton Manor Community Primary School, Sutton Manor

The Five Rings

At night I had a dream about the weirdest things.
On my bed were five spinning rings.
The rings were a portal to a magic place,
Where you and your pet lion can race.
Make sure he doesn't roar in your face.
Next we move on to Candy Land, a land so imaginative.

Ethan Marsh (9)
Sutton Manor Community Primary School, Sutton Manor

A Very Random Dream

I go upstairs and get in bed,
Time to visit inside my head,
Up in the sky where the stars glow,
"Oh, look up there!" Away I go,
I get right up and on my feet,
High in the sky, where the stars meet,
Way up there, where the room dances,
And the darkness' ominous glances.

There are lots of random things,
Like a table that always sings,
Or a giant walking talking book,
I guess that's just some weird luck.
Up in the sky is a nice rainbow,
And a kangaroo that will sometimes glow,
And as far as I'm aware,
There's even a whispering chair!

The list just goes on and on,
There's also a pencil that's always gone.

Joseph Hanson (11)
West Denton Primary School, West Denton

An Encounter With Henry VIII

I don't know where I am,
He wasn't eating much but clam.
There he was, Henry VIII,
It looked like he was planning something with his mate.
He must have been divorcing his wife,
I don't know how this doesn't ruin his life.

Wife number two is on the way,
This seems like an awful game he dares to play.
Although he is a powerful Tudor monarch,
He chopped her head off when the sky was dark.
Then he had another wife,
One that he truly loved,
And she dropped dead when little Edward was birthed.

He married another three,
But I actually woke up,
Before I got to see.

Casey Reynolds (11)
West Denton Primary School, West Denton

The Kind Woman

Walking around, nowhere to go
I see other people with their loved ones
I got nothing new to wear this Christmas
For I have no one that loves me

As I walk as long as my legs can carry me
I stumble upon a tall, wooden castle
The surroundings are not welcoming
There are bones and skeletons everywhere

I decide to go inside
Because it is cold outside
As I enter the castle, I see a woman
She is ever so kind

She gives me clothes to wear
And food to devour
Oh, she is the kindest woman ever
And I shall love her forever

In dreams we find what we desire.

Jaklyn Elizabeth Jinto (11)
West Denton Primary School, West Denton

The Agent's Secret

An agent told me a secret,
It was impossible to keep it,
I went and told my friend,
Now he wants to put me to an end,
I was in danger,
I was being chased by a stranger.

I don't know how I got into this mess,
It's not the first time I guess,
I get chased all the time,
I don't even have a dime.
People might think I look rich,
Trust me, I wish.

More agents appeared,
One had a very long beard,
I felt like I was being chased by angry geese,
I was about to ring the police!
It was the fastest I've ever ran,
Even faster than a van.

Denver Bell (11)
West Denton Primary School, West Denton

That One Time I Was A Chair

I once had a dream,
A rather peculiar dream.
I was a chair,
For I was a spare,
For a rather large company,
Which was based on a colony.
I had a rivalry with a table,
Who worked in a stable.
He was in quite a bit of agony,
Because he had lost his balcony,
Because it had been stolen,
By a man who had some tokens!

It may not make much sense,
But if you had two pence,
You might have bought a fence,
Or you'd be silenced,
By someone who was balanced!

I used to have a friend,
He did not want to offend.

Harley Mitchell (11)
West Denton Primary School, West Denton

A Little Trapped In The Dream

In my dreams every night,
A girl wanders through a forest every night,
Crunch, crunch, crunch,
As I step onto the leaves,
Tap, tap, tap,
As I walk into the maze,
I hear the sound,
Bang, bang, bang,
I'm scared to step forwards,
So maybe not right now,
But why am I thinking this?
Will I wake up from my nightmare?
Bang, bang, bang,
It is starting to close up,
I don't know if I will last a minute,
Or even a second,
In my dream.

Lola Jones (10)
West Denton Primary School, West Denton

Monsters: In Your Dreams!

What is it I see?
Oh no, it could not be,
Creeping up beside me,
Creeping up behind me,
How long have they been planning this?
I'm so scared, is this it?

I snap back to bed,
Wondering what's going on in my head.
But I know there is something,
I felt it moving and thumping,
I go back to sleep,
But now I have the creeps!

This can not be real,
I could end up in a meal,
Let me say goodbye,
Or maybe bye-bye,
What do I do?
This can not be true!

Evie Richmond-Atkin (10)
West Denton Primary School, West Denton

The Black Hole

I don't know where I am,
I don't want to know,
All my fears are here,
Like clowns, spiders and monsters,
In the night,
I am terrified and
I want to go home,
Wait!
Look, there's Anne Boleyn,
Maybe she knows
What is going on.

Evil clowns chasing,
Anne calls for me,
Begging me to come,
Little do I know,
A shape-shifter awaits,
Disguised,
Devilish eyes and scales appear,
Then I pinch myself and find out,
It was just a nightmare.

Leila Birkett (11)
West Denton Primary School, West Denton

Nightmares

Fall asleep and let your imagination shine,
Some are too long,
Some are too short,
Some are scary,
Asleep in a dark hallway,
Full of doors in my dream,
Each door hides a tale,
I wake up and fall,
The doors are whistling like the wind,
I choose a random door to explore,
Walking freely through a forest,
Each tree is as tall as each other,
Whisper coming from everywhere,
I am so scared,
What shall I do?
I fall over the root of a tree,
And I wake up in my bed.

Charlie Johnston (11)
West Denton Primary School, West Denton

Dreams: Magical Things

Dreams, oh dreams,
Such magical things,
Whether you're floating through space,
Or eating a giant gorilla-shaped cake!
Dreams are beautiful,
Each one so unique,
Your imagination runs free,
Each time you drift off to sleep.

Riding a bus to the moon,
That sounds pretty cool!
Meeting aliens,
That go to your school,
Or finding a unicorn,
That's six foot tall,
Dreams have it all!

You can be anyone,
Even Taylor Swift!
You can be anything.

Sophie Thompson (11)
West Denton Primary School, West Denton

Boom! Bang! Pop!

Boom! Bang! Pop!
Extraordinary colours filled the night
Smiles filled our faces
New year is here!

Breathtaking and thrilling
The enchanting colours pulled us in
Take my hand and trust

Boom! Bang! Pop!
Balls of fire danced up into the darkness
Fireworks went supernova
They made you feel alive!
Fireworks came as God's graffiti

Whizz!
There went the last explosion
The last of the screams
It was all a dream.

Sophia Calvert (10)
West Denton Primary School, West Denton

Out

Fly high in the sky.
Out of space we die,
I do not know where we are,
Are we on a different planet?

It is not Earth, is it?
I don't know what it is,
Not a normal planet,
It's just not Earth.
It has over 8,955 aliens.

Then I land on the mysterious planet,
It is far away from Earth.
In seconds my house is built,
Am I in time?
And the aliens beep bop, they say, "How are you?"

Alfie Grey (10)
West Denton Primary School, West Denton

Invisible Me

Walking around in a lonely street,
With nowhere to go and no one to see,
Surrounded by people all around,
Feeling unnoticed all year round!
Invisible me.

Thinking of the bright sides,
I would be in peace outside,
Watch the pantomime every year,
Always moving here and there,
Invisible me.

Unfortunately, I will be unseen,
Forever it shall be,
Invisible me.

Omasirichim Oparah (11)
West Denton Primary School, West Denton

I Never Knew My Garden Was So Weird

I don't know,
As I said next to the back door,
It was a scary spartan,
That shouted Martin,
The spartan ran,
Only to find a fan.

Whoosh!
The bee turned on the fan.
But fans were banned in my country,
How was it there,
Was it a bear?

The grass began to dance,
And then it had a trance,
What were the chances that grass could dance?

Layton Ellis (11)
West Denton Primary School, West Denton

Tap, Tap, Tap

Waiting and wondering, I stare,
Suddenly I see an awful glare,
I thought it was my friend, so I said hey,
But then this glare asked if I would play.

Tap, tap, tap, I hear,
But what's stopping me from listening is,
The ringing in my ear,
With the tapping getting louder, I scream,
And I wake up and realise it was just a silly dream,
Or was it real?

Rosie Rooney (11)
West Denton Primary School, West Denton

Floating Through Space

Floating through space,
The mysterious planets stand out,
Oh, how it's such a wonderful place!
They are so beautiful, you must agree!
Jupiter, Venus and Mars stand out to me!
Like an antique vase, they are unique.
Oh no, my spaceship is beginning to creak,
Plummeting to Earth, I am so scared.
What is to come?
For what is next, I am unprepared.

Jake Stoddart (11)
West Denton Primary School, West Denton

A Strange World

At first, I was paralysed with fear,
Then I felt like I belonged here.
There were fairies that wanted to steal your teeth,
Griffins that could sweep you off your feet,
Trees could walk, flowers could talk,
There were witches and ghouls,
And you can't forget the acid pools,
Some people may say, this place is horrifying,
But to me, it's electrifying.

Katie McGuinness (11)
West Denton Primary School, West Denton

I Dream Of Burgers

It was an ordinary afternoon,
The sun was shining and I saw it,
It made me much more hungry,
I couldn't wait to eat!
When I tried to take a bite,
The burger slapped me twice,
It took my wallet out of my pocket,
And it ran away.
I chased outside,
Only to find,
Thousands of walking burgers,
Am I going out of my mind?

Yafee Ahmed (11)
West Denton Primary School, West Denton

Switched Lives

I was in the sky, flying high,
Then I realised I switched my life,
I was a pilot flying over the many blue seas,
Then I saw a big hippo like a block of cheese.

I tried to escape this weird dream,
I steered left and right, with all of my might,
I landed in one of the holes, *splat!*
I woke up in my bed.

Freddie Coulson (10)
West Denton Primary School, West Denton

In My Nightmare, There's A Monster Hiding Under My Bed

I know he's there,
And he knows I'm there waiting for me to get out of bed,
He's ready to pounce
And grab me with his tentacles.
I hear his distorted noises,
I feel a cold shiver rushing
Down my spine.
I see red glowing eyes
Staring right into my soul.
Suddenly, it pounces,
I wake up.

Leo Dunn (9)
West Denton Primary School, West Denton

Nightmares

Nightmares,
Some come true,
Some don't.

Nightmares,
Some are scary,
Some can and can't.

Nightmares,
Some can be long,
Some can't.

Nightmares,
Some you can scream,
Some you can't.

Mine came true,
It was too scary, I couldn't tell you.

Freya Ions (11)
West Denton Primary School, West Denton

Drifting Out In Space Time

All I see is a beautiful night.
I see stars glaring upon Earth, it just makes me mesmerised.
As I go up higher I can see a colourful galaxy that appears in space time.
I see big and small stars and I wonder if there are more...

I can see different planets, Venus and Mars,
And I know there is much more to explore.

Frazer Branscombe (11)
West Denton Primary School, West Denton

Football Horror

My heart is beating loudly,
I woke up in a mysterious place,
A grassy area, I don't know where,
Surrounded, trapped, but wait...
I recognise this place,
A stadium, a dream come true,
There are enemies upon us.
They are coming for me,
I try to run,
I am getting carried,
Help! Help! Help!

Mason Barwick (11)
West Denton Primary School, West Denton

Magnificent Dragon

In my nightmare, deep in a cave,
Where it's dark and silent,
Lives a magnificent dragon.
His eyes are like black coal.
Blinding scales hurt my eyes.

He is never violent but,
Don't anger the beast
Or beg for mercy you will.
In my nightmare, deep in a cave,
Lives a magnificent dragon.

Ahmed Ayalu (10)
West Denton Primary School, West Denton

Dreams

Dreams,
Some are so big,
Some are so small.

Dreams,
Some come true,
Some sadly don't.

Dreams,
Some are too long,
Some are too short.

Dreams,
Some are fun,
Some are scary.

Mine was scary,
Too scary, I can't explain.

Darci Jones (11)
West Denton Primary School, West Denton

The Maze

I woke up, surrounded by six big walls that reached up to Mars,
As I got out of bed,
The walls began to move,
Running through the strange maze,
My heart started to beat with adrenaline and fear,
I woke up,
And it was all a dream.

David Sager (10)
West Denton Primary School, West Denton

Creeping Up On You

C hasing, walking and following you,
R ealising there's nothing there,
E ating up the food, while you're not there,
E erie sounds in your house,
P oking you when asleep,
I nside, outside, everywhere there's frightening noises,
N ervously panicking from your heart to soul,
G iant footsteps bigger than mountains.

U p I go on the giant stairs, I hear the door but there's no one there,
P lacing my hands over my eyes,

O pening my eyes and seeing the daylight,
N othing there, but am I sure?

Y ellow sun, grey clouds, lots of noises but not loud,
O n my head, I felt a little touch,
U pon waking, I only just notice, it was all just a dream, or was it?

Gabi Sidoli (10)
Whitestone Primary School, Swansea

Fantastic Football Game

In my dreams, I like to play football on grass,
I want to win, I don't want to come last.
A good team is what I need,
My dog will help me, he has super speed.
His name is Piper, he may be small,
But he is the best footballer of them all.
I feel nervous in my stomach but also excited,
If my dog scores, he will be delighted!
With the ball at my feet, I'm starting to aim,
Trying to make the pass to win the game.
Dodging the defender who's a kicker and a swiper,
The ball lands precisely in front of Piper.
He grunts and growls as he tries to shoot,
The ball flies past the goalkeeper's boot.
Goal! I'm ecstatic, we've won as a team,
I woke up so happy, was it a dream?

Judah Scott (11)
Whitestone Primary School, Swansea

Peaceful World

P eople laughing and having lots of fun.
E nergy spreads throughout the world.
A ngry people are no more.
C alming sensations spreading like Nutella.
E cstatic expressions on everyone's faces.
F antastic friends surrounding me.
U tterly amazing world it is.
L oving each other each day with all our hearts.

W onderful people helping each other in harmony.
O ur planet without borders!
R ainbows filling the sky from top to bottom like a kaleidoscope of colour.
L aughter from children echoing around our Earth.
D ancing all together, full of joy and happiness.

Dakota Mitchell (10)
Whitestone Primary School, Swansea

My Odd Nightmare

I opened my eyes to see a river full of blood. I looked around, only to see a scarlet wave emerge from the blood-filled river. The wave submerged me and my body began to feel sticky as I fought for breath in the bloody river.

Just then, a large swan poked its head out. My eyes opened wide with fear as the swan swam towards me, its mouth open like a black hole, only with razor-sharp teeth. Its fangs grew larger and larger. I ducked into the scarlet water for protection, but the swan was right above my head. It sank down to engulf me whole.

What sort of nightmare was that? I thought with a shudder.

Gwen Stephens (9)
Whitestone Primary School, Swansea

A Crazy Dream

O nce upon a dream a big,
N asty
C rocodile came out of a boy's bed,
E ating all his bread.

U nderneath the boy's bed was a
P ig eating hay!
O n the boy's shelf was a
N asty little worm digging through his clay!

A nd then there was a

D eer galloping across the room,
R ight then a bird came flying with a broom,
E nough! The horrified boy cried,
A huge creature crept out of the wardrobe,
M onster attack!

Rajan Parmar (10)
Whitestone Primary School, Swansea

Once Upon A Dream

In the middle of the deep blue sea,
Is a sailing ship, black as black can be.
She's called the Skull Hunter,
Her stories known only to the fish under.

So many guns pointing out,
Ready to sink ships, all in one bout.
Masts as high as coconut trees,
Holding sails that catch the breeze.

A black flag with skull and bones,
"Run away if you can," it warns.
The famous pirate captain Blackbeard,
Runs this ship that's notorious and feared.

Prabash Dissanayake (10)
Whitestone Primary School, Swansea

Spiders

S cary, hairy spiders crawling around,
P eeping through the gaps, running across the ground,
I n the wardrobe, there's a big, giant spider,
D on't go near there or get a scare,
E yes looking all around, try not to make a sound,
R unning freely across the floor, you better not open that door,
S oon, it may eat me unless I close that wardrobe door.

Lilly Bromham (11)
Whitestone Primary School, Swansea

Afterlife

My dreams come true,
The shining star and me meet again
Wagging tails and licks saying, "Hello again."
My heart exploding with love.
Our favourite place is full again.
The salty sea splashing, seagulls whirling round.
Our noses taking in the smells.
A flash of hope but my eyes are flickering.
Waking up, it disappears.
My star is gone again.

Nell Taylor (11)
Whitestone Primary School, Swansea

Spiders

In my dreams,
Or nightmares, I should say,
Spiders crawl about my face,
Hairy legs in all directions,
Shooting cobwebs.
I have no protection,
Hitting, kicking, screaming,
As I wake in bed,
Soundly safe,
With a face full of dread.

Lamar Haj Basheer (11)
Whitestone Primary School, Swansea

Dream

D ancers floating on pink clouds,
R ainbows paint colours on them as they pass,
E ven the clouds look like pink candyfloss,
A ll the dancers smile and laugh,
M y brain in the clouds.

Ella Evans (10)
Whitestone Primary School, Swansea

YOUNG WRITERS INFORMATION

We hope you have enjoyed reading this book – and that you will continue to in the coming years.

If you're a young writer who enjoys reading and creative writing, or the parent of an enthusiastic poet or story writer, do visit our website **www.youngwriters.co.uk**. Here you will find free competitions, workshops and games, as well as recommended reads, a poetry glossary and our blog.

If you would like to order further copies of this book, or any of our other titles, then please give us a call or visit **www.youngwriters.co.uk**.

Young Writers
Remus House
Coltsfoot Drive
Peterborough
PE2 9BF
(01733) 890066
info@youngwriters.co.uk

YoungWritersUK   YoungWritersCW
youngwriterscw   youngwriterscw